THE AMERICAN
IDENTITY

by Jill Sherman

Content Consultant
Richard Bell
Associate Professor, Department of History
University of Maryland

Core Library

An Imprint of Abdo Publishing
abdopublishing.com

abdopublishing.com

Published by Abdo Publishing, a division of ABDO, PO Box 398166, Minneapolis, Minnesota 55439. Copyright © 2017 by Abdo Consulting Group, Inc. International copyrights reserved in all countries. No part of this book may be reproduced in any form without written permission from the publisher. Core Library™ is a trademark and logo of Abdo Publishing.

Printed in the United States of America, North Mankato, Minnesota
032016
092016

THIS BOOK CONTAINS
RECYCLED MATERIALS

Cover Photo: Andrea Izzotti/Shutterstock Images
Interior Photos: Andrea Izzotti/Shutterstock Images, 1; Tetra Images/Corbis, 4, 43; Pictorial Press Ltd/Alamy, 7; Susan Montoya/AP Images, 8; MaxFX/Shutterstock Images, 12, 45; NASA, 15 (top left); Joe Rosenthal/AP Images, 15 (bottom left); 2001 The Record(Bergen Co. NJ/)/Getty Images, 15 (right); Matej Hudovernik/Shutterstock Images, 17; Lionel Hahn/Sipa USA/AP Images, 18; Haraz N. Ghanbari/AP Images, 24; Oli Scarff/iStockphoto, 27; Shutterstock Images, 29 (top row, left); iStockphoto, 29; Kent Weakley/Shutterstock Images, 30; Critterbiz/Shutterstock Images, 33; David Drapkin/AP Images, 36; Joe Seer/Shutterstock Images, 39

Editor: Sharon F. Doorasamy
Series Designer: Laura Polzin

Cataloging-in-Publication Data
Names: Sherman, Jill, author.
Title: The American identity / by Jill Sherman.
Description: Minneapolis, MN : Abdo Publishing, [2017] | Series: American
    citizenship | Includes bibliographical references and index.
Identifiers: LCCN 2015960482 | ISBN 9781680782394 (lib. bdg.) |
    ISBN 9781680776508 (ebook)
Subjects: LCSH: United States--History--Juvenile literature. | Emblems, National-
    -United States--Juvenile literature. | Signs and symbols--United States--
    Juvenile literature.
Classification: DDC 973--dc23
LC record available at http://lccn.loc.gov/2015960482

CONTENTS

CHAPTER ONE

WHO ARE WE?

American identity is shaped by the nation's history. This history dates back to the Declaration of Independence and the US Constitution. These documents express what it means to be an American. American identity is also expressed in symbols, landmarks, and traditions.

The US Constitution on top of the American flag

History and Identity

Thirteen American colonies gained their independence from Britain in 1776. The Declaration of Independence lays out their reasons for wanting to separate. It also outlines their basic beliefs. One belief is that "all men are created equal." Another is that people have the right to a happy life.

Prominent men wrote the Declaration of Independence. These doctors, lawyers, farmers, and politicians are known as the Founding Fathers. When writing the document, women, African Americans, and Native Americans were not foremost in their minds. However, the document they created came to represent the new nation's ideals.

The Founding Fathers

The Founding Fathers helped to shape American identity. But like all people, they were not perfect. Thomas Jefferson wrote "all men are created equal" in the Declaration of Independence. Yet, like many people of his time, he owned slaves.

The John Trumbull painting *Declaration of Independence* shows the presentation of a draft of the famous document.

A Nation of Immigrants

The United States is a nation of immigrants. People of any race or religion can be American. The country

Native American dancers at the annual Gathering of Nations

is often called a melting pot. Immigrants come to the United States seeking a better life.

Some people came to America unwillingly, though. The first African people arrived in 1619. They were enslaved. Slaves suffered in America for more than 200 years. Only after the American Civil War (1861–1865) was slavery outlawed.

Early European settlers in North America did not arrive on an empty landscape. Native Americans lived throughout the continent. Settlers took land from Native Americans. This led to clashes. By the 1800s, the US government

PERSPECTIVES
A Weakening Identity

Some Americans worry that the country's national identity is weakening. They worry about immigration. Immigration became a topic of debate during the 2016 presidential campaign. The candidates held different views. Some favored sending illegal immigrants back to their home countries. Others suggested ways to allow them to stay legally in the United States.

had pushed Native Americans into areas called reservations.

The United States was founded on the idea of freedom and equality. Some groups have protested and battled in courts to gain their full rights as Americans. But the ideals expressed in the Declaration of Independence have remained unchanged. They have given hope of a better life to all Americans throughout the nation's history.

James Truslow Adams wrote a 1931 book titled *The Epic of America*. In it, he describes his view of the American Dream:

> [The American Dream is] that dream of a land in which life should be better and richer and fuller for everyone, with opportunity for each according to ability or achievement. It is a difficult dream for the European upper classes to interpret adequately, and too many of us ourselves have grown weary and mistrustful of it. It is not a dream of motor cars and high wages merely, but a dream of social order in which each man and each woman shall be able to attain to the fullest stature of which they are innately capable, and be recognized by others for what they are, regardless of the fortuitous circumstances of birth or position.

> Source: "The American Dream." Library of Congress. *Library of Congress*, n.d. Web. Accessed January 28, 2016.

What's the Big Idea?

Read the words carefully. What is the author's main idea? What details from this text best show the author's purpose?

CHAPTER TWO

SYMBOLS OF THE UNITED STATES

Most Americans can name symbols of the United States. They may know the US flag, the Statue of Liberty, or Uncle Sam. These symbols are powerful. They are meant to inspire pride among Americans. US citizens often rally behind the nation's symbols.

American flags

Old Glory

People around the world know the US flag. It is known as the "Stars and Stripes" or "Old Glory." In 1777, the leaders of the 13 American colonies agreed to create a flag. They decided it would have 13 stripes alternating between red and white. They placed 13 white stars on a blue background in the upper left corner. In 1818, Congress began adding a star for each new state. The current US flag has 50 stars.

Lady Liberty and Uncle Sam

The Statue of Liberty has welcomed generations of immigrants to the United States. The statue is also

Flag Maker Betsy Ross

Many Americans believe that Betsy Ross made the first American flag. There is no proof of this claim, though. One of Ross's grandsons made the claim in 1870. That was almost 100 years after she had supposedly sewn it. In 1893 an artist painted a portrait of Ross. The flag is on her lap. It became a famous image. The Philadelphia seamstress did make flags. But historians have found no proof of her grandson's claims.

US astronauts Neil Armstrong and Edwin E. "Buzz" Aldrin plant a US flag on the moon.

Terrorists attacked the United States on September 11, 2001. Firefighters raised a US flag over the rubble as they worked.

Marines raise a US flag atop the Japanese island Iwo Jima during the closing months of World War II.

Raising the American Flag

The US flag appears in many famous photos of important events in US history. Take a look at these photographs. How does the flag add meaning to each image?

PERSPECTIVES
Flag Burning

In 1984, Gregory Lee Johnson burned the American flag. It was his way to protest. He disagreed with President Ronald Reagan's policies. Johnson was arrested. However, Johnson believed his right to free speech protected his act. The case made its way to the Supreme Court. In 1989, the court ruled in his favor in *Texas v. Johnson*. Justice Anthony Kennedy explained his feeling about the ruling:

> *The flag is constant in expressing beliefs Americans share, beliefs in law and peace and that freedom which sustains the human spirit. . . . It is poignant but fundamental that the flag protects those who hold it in contempt.*

known as Lady Liberty. Completed in 1886, it was a gift from the French people. It symbolizes friendship between the two nations. It stands in New York Harbor. Many immigrants arrived by boat. The statue was the first American landmark they saw.

Uncle Sam is a symbol for the US government. He is known for his white hair and beard. He appeared on military recruitment posters during World War I (1914–1918) and World War II (1939–1945).

The Statue of Liberty is one of New York's most popular tourist attractions.

SHOWING PATRIOTISM

Patriotism is love for one's country. It unites a nation's people. Reciting the Pledge of Allegiance is meant to inspire feelings of patriotism. So is the singing of the national anthem, "The Star-Spangled Banner."

The Pledge

Baptist minister Francis Bellamy wrote the Pledge of Allegiance in 1892. It celebrated the 400th anniversary

Pop singer Lady Gaga performs the national anthem at the Super Bowl in February 2016.

of Christopher Columbus's arrival in the Americas. Bellamy believed the pledge was important. The American Civil War was still a recent memory. The pledge was meant to unite the nation under one flag. It originally read: "I pledge allegiance to my flag and the Republic for which it stands—one Nation indivisible—with liberty and justice for all."

The words to the pledge have changed over the years. The meaning remains the same. People regularly recite it at schools and at public gatherings.

PERSPECTIVES
Under God

The phrase "under God" was not originally part of the Pledge of Allegiance. Congress approved those words in 1954. A Catholic organization suggested the change. The proposal didn't get much support at first. Then President Dwight D. Eisenhower heard his pastor use the words in a sermon. Eisenhower got behind the proposal. Congress passed it. In the 1950s, the United States' major rival was the Soviet Union. The communist nation opposed religion. The change to the pledge drew a sharp line between the two nations.

National Anthem

Francis Scott Key wrote the words to the US national anthem. He originally wrote it as a poem during the War of 1812 (1812–1815). Key watched the British Navy's attack on Fort McHenry in Baltimore, Maryland. This was on the night of September 13, 1814. The smoke finally cleared in the morning. Key saw that the American flag still flew over the fort. He was overcome by emotion. He wrote his poem, "Defence of Fort McHenry."

The poem was later set to music. It was published under the name "The Star-Spangled Banner." The song became hugely

Famous Performances

Countless artists have performed "The Star-Spangled Banner." Jennifer Hudson, Carrie Underwood, and Beyoncé have all given great performances. But the most famous was Whitney Houston's solo at the 1991 Super Bowl. Her version gained popularity again following the September 11, 2001, terrorist attacks on the United States.

popular. "The Star-Spangled Banner" officially became the national anthem on March 3, 1931. It is sung at a wide variety of public events.

Americans are expected to stand when the anthem plays. Men's hats are supposed to come off. People are expected to face the flag. Then, they are supposed to put their right hand over their heart. Members of the military can salute instead.

FURTHER EVIDENCE

Chapter Three talks about patriotism. What is one of the main points of this chapter? What evidence is included to support this point? Read the article at the website below. Does the information on the website support the main point of the chapter? Does it present new evidence?

How Do You Define Patriotism?
mycorelibrary.com/american-identity

The original Star-Spangled Banner was about one-fourth the size of a modern basketball court. The flag was meant to be visible from great distances. Given its size and splendor, it is no wonder that Francis Scott Key was inspired to pen his famous words:

O say can you see, by the dawn's early light,
What so proudly we hail'd at the twilight's last gleaming,
Whose broad stripes and bright stars through the perilous
fight
O'er the ramparts we watch'd were so gallantly streaming?
And the rocket's red glare, the bombs bursting in air,
Gave proof through the night that our flag was still there,
O say does that star-spangled banner yet wave
O'er the land of the free and the home of the brave?

Source: "The Star-Spangled Banner." Fort McHenry. National Park Service, January 28, 2016. Web. Accessed January 28, 2016

Consider Your Audience

Review the lyrics closely. Consider how to change them for a modern audience. Rewrite the lyrics so that your friends can understand them. How does your new version differ from the original text, and why?

CHAPTER FOUR

CELEBRATING THE AMERICAN WAY

Holidays are a time for celebration. Many holidays are religious. Most countries also have their own national holidays. The United States is no different. Ten federal holidays are celebrated in the United States. Several relate to American heritage.

Fireworks light up the night sky on Independence Day in the nation's capital.

The Story of Thanksgiving

Not all Americans celebrate Thanksgiving Day. Some Native Americans object to the holiday. They participate in an annual protest. They point to the fact that Americans killed Native Americans, stole their land, and put them on reservations. Protest leader Mahtowin Munro calls the traditional story of Thanksgiving "a fantasy history:"

> All around the country, schools continue to dress up their children in little Pilgrim and Indian costumes and the Indians welcome the Pilgrims and they all sit down together. . . . That's not at all what happened.

Celebrating History

Independence Day is celebrated on July 4. It is considered the country's birthday. The date marks the adoption of the Declaration of Independence on July 4, 1776. People enjoy picnics and cookouts to observe the day. They fly the flag and cheer at patriotic parades. At night, fireworks light up skies above cities.

Thanksgiving Day is celebrated on the fourth Thursday in November. It pays tribute to a meal

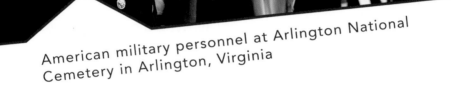

American military personnel at Arlington National Cemetery in Arlington, Virginia

between early settlers and Native Americans in 1621. It has been celebrated since 1863. Most Americans spend Thanksgiving with family and friends. They traditionally eat turkey, stuffing, cranberry sauce, and pumpkin pie.

Honoring the Military

Two holidays pay tribute to members of the US military. Veterans Day honors people who have served in the military. It occurs on November 11. The holiday was created after World War I (1914–1918). Many other nations that fought in the war also observe this date with special tributes.

Memorial Day is the last Monday of May. This holiday honors those who have died in military service. It started during the Civil War. The day became a national holiday in 1971. Americans watch parades and visit cemeteries and memorials. They may leave flowers to honor a family member who died.

The Thanksgiving Turkey

In 1963 President John F. Kennedy spared the life of a Thanksgiving turkey. Every US president since Kennedy has followed his example and let a turkey go free. This relatively new tradition is known as the annual presidential turkey pardon.

Remembering Workers

Labor Day is another important holiday. In the 1800s, workers faced unsafe conditions. They often worked

American Holidays

Take a close look at the ten official US holidays listed in the chart above. Consider why some Americans may not like certain holidays such as Christmas and Columbus Day. Explain the reasons in your own words.

12-hour days. Children worked in factories. Labor unions worked to pass laws to protect workers. This led to shorter workdays and safer conditions. The idea for a holiday for working people became popular. It became a national holiday in 1894. Labor Day is celebrated on the first Monday of September.

CHAPTER FIVE

SYMBOLIC PLACES

The United States is rich with landmarks. Many are located in the nation's capital, Washington, DC. One is the White House, where the president lives. Another is the Capitol, the meeting place of the US Congress. Washington, DC, also has memorials to honor Presidents Abraham Lincoln and Thomas Jefferson. The Vietnam Veterans Memorial is there too.

The Lincoln Memorial at sunrise in Washington, DC

It honors the soldiers who fought in the Vietnam War (1954–1975).

One of the city's most colorful landmarks is its collection of cherry trees. The mayor of Tokyo, Japan, gave them to the city in 1912. The trees attract many visitors to the National Cherry Blossom Festival. It is held in March each year.

State Landmarks

Other landmarks are spread across the country. Philadelphia, Pennsylvania, displays the Liberty Bell. California has the Golden Gate Bridge. South Dakota

National Parks

The United States has more than 400 national parks. The parks cover more than 84 million acres (34 million hectares). In 1872, Yellowstone National Park became the world's first national park. It spans 3,472 square miles (8,992 sq km) in Idaho, Montana, and Wyoming. President Theodore Roosevelt was a great supporter of national parks. During his eight years as president (1901–09), more than 100 million acres (40 million hectares) of forest were set aside for protection.

Nearly 3 million people visit Mount Rushmore each year.

Remembering the Alamo

Richard Flores is a professor at the University of Texas. He noticed that not everyone saw the Alamo as a place of pride. Many of his Mexican-American and Latino friends show mixed and hostile feelings toward the place.

What explains this? Mexicans won the battle at the Alamo. However, they dislike Antonio López de Santa Anna. He led the battle. Santa Anna is seen as a villain. The Mexican general is blamed for losing Texas. Schoolbooks in Mexico rarely mention the Alamo.

attracts visitors to Mount Rushmore National Memorial. This stone carving honors four American presidents. They are George Washington, Thomas Jefferson, Theodore Roosevelt, and Abraham Lincoln.

Texas is home to the Alamo. This fort is famous as the site of an 1836 battle. Texans defended the fort against Mexican soldiers. At the time, Texas was not part of the United States. It was part of Mexico. In 1829, Mexico banned slavery. But the colonists living there wanted to preserve slavery. So the colonists decided to fight for independence from Mexico.

The Texans were outnumbered and defeated. A month and a half later, Texans attacked the Mexican Army in revenge at the Battle of San Jacinto. They shouted, "Remember the Alamo." Though it is a site of a lost battle, it was a turning point in the war. The phrase "Remember the Alamo" is still heard in popular culture today.

CHAPTER SIX

AMERICAN CULTURE

C ulture is made up of the shared experience of a group of people. It includes history, symbols, values, religion, food, sports, and industry. It also includes the arts, including music, TV shows, movies, and literature. The United States is a rich mix of many cultures. This diversity drives American invention and achievement.

Millions of American sports fans love to cheer for their favorite teams.

The Land of Many Cultures

Each state and region has its own cultural influences. There is Mardi Gras, an annual carnival celebration in New Orleans, Louisiana. In New York, there's the Brooklyn Hip-Hop Festival. The festival celebrates hip-hop music and culture. Park City, Utah, has the Sundance Film Festival. It is the largest independent film festival in the United States.

American Movies

Hollywood is a big industry. It produces blockbuster movies seen in theaters all over the world. American movies are influential to many places abroad. French film director Jean-Jacques Annaud said, "America is the only country capable of producing national movies: its culture has become global culture."

American cuisine combines many cultural and regional influences. Grits and chopped barbecue, for example, are found in the South. Shoofly pie is a classic dessert of the Amish of Pennsylvania and Ohio. Tex-Mex is cuisine influenced by Tejano culture. Tejanos are Texans

Taylor Swift at the 2013 American Music Awards in Los Angeles, California

of Spanish or Mexican heritage. They lived in Texas before it became a republic.

Pop Culture and Beyond

Hollywood movies, TV shows, and music greatly influence American identity. Jazz, bluegrass, country, rap, rhythm and blues, rock and roll, and hip-hop are all American sounds. From Elvis Presley and Chuck Berry in the 1950s to Kanye West and Carrie Underwood today, American artists represent US culture.

American television and films are also influential. Shows such as *Sesame Street* are broadcast around the globe. Movie stars such as Jennifer Lawrence, Will Smith, and Robert Downey Jr. are household names.

Americans also love their sports, especially football, basketball, and baseball. Its players are icons. Tom Brady is famous for football. LeBron James is admired for basketball. Babe Ruth and Jackie Robinson are baseball legends.

The cultural influence of American business is also enormous. It extends to people and places around the world. McDonald's, Coca-Cola, Disney, the iPhone, Twitter, and Ford are widely known brand names in the United States and abroad.

American identity is rooted in US history and its people. It continues to evolve. Each generation contributes new ideas. Each generation also works to ensure the United States lives up to the ideals in its founding documents. American symbols, landmarks, and culture are ever-present reminders of these ideals.

EXPLORE ONLINE

Foreign students often study in the United States. Parts of US culture are known around the world. Other parts will be new to them. They may find it difficult to understand American customs. Student exchange programs help. They share information about US culture. Visit the website below. How well does this site prepare students for life in the United States?

American Culture
mycorelibrary.com/american-identity

FAST FACTS

- The American flag is a highly recognizable US symbol. Americans honor the flag to show respect for the flag and the country.
- Reciting the Pledge of Allegiance at schools and public gatherings is intended to build a sense of belonging and community.
- The US national anthem is the "The Star-Spangled Banner." It is often played before sports events and government celebrations.
- Independence Day celebrates the adoption of the Declaration of Independence in 1776.
- Veterans Day honors all members of the military, and Memorial Day honors soldiers who died during wartime.
- The nation's capital, Washington, DC, is home to many US landmarks.

- The Statue of Liberty was a gift from the French people and symbolizes friendship and freedom.
- George Washington, Thomas Jefferson, Theodore Roosevelt, and Abraham Lincoln are carved into Mount Rushmore in South Dakota.
- American music and movies influence how people abroad perceive the United States.

STOP AND THINK

Say What?

Studying American identity can mean learning new vocabulary. Find five words in this book you've never heard before. Use a dictionary to find out what they mean. Then write the meanings in your own words, and use each word in a new sentence.

Tell the Tale

Chapter Three describes how Francis Scott Key was inspired to write the national anthem. Imagine you were an eyewitness to the attack on Fort McHenry by the British. Describe what it was like to see the flag still flying after the bombardment. Write 200 words about the experience.

Dig Deeper

After reading this book, what questions do you still have about American identity? With an adult's help, find a few reliable sources that can help you answer your questions. Write a paragraph about what you learned.

Surprise Me

Chapter Six talks about American culture. Culture includes music, fashion, art, sports, and movies. After reading this chapter, what two or three facts did you find most surprising? Write a few sentences about each idea or fact. Why did you find each idea or fact surprising?

GLOSSARY

communist
a person who believes in a system of government in which all factories, farms, land, and natural resources are owned by the government

constitution
a document that describes the system of beliefs and laws that govern a state or country

fortuitous
happening by chance

immigrants
people who have come to live in a new country

interpret
to explain the meaning of something

social order
the way that society is organized

stature
level of respect for achievement

veteran
someone who has fought in a war

LEARN MORE

Books

Kelley, True. *Where Is Mount Rushmore?* New York: Grosset & Dunlap, 2015.

King, David C. *Children's Encyclopedia of American History*. New York: DK Publishing, in association with the Smithsonian Institution, 2014.

Websites

To learn more about American Citizenship, visit **booklinks.abdopublishing.com**. These links are routinely monitored and updated to provide the most current information available.

Visit **mycorelibrary.com** for free additional tools for teachers and students.

INDEX

ABOUT THE AUTHOR

Jill Sherman lives and writes in Brooklyn, New York. She has written over a dozen books for young people. She enjoys researching new topics and is thrilled to be sharing the meaning of the American experience with young readers.